MY HEART STILL BEATS

My Soul awakens....

My Heart still beats....

Anyway.

Nancy Hoppes Sellnau

Edited By: Edit This One, LLC., Fairfax, IA.
www.editthisone.com

Published By: Edit This One, LLC d/b/a Wordy Gerty Publishing.

Wordy Gerty
Publishing

Cover and back cover designs created by MacKenzie Sellnau. Turtle design created by Greg Bordignon.

ISBN: 978-0-9981046-7-6

Table of Contents

Dedication

Dedicated to the memories....and all who made them possible by sharing my journey. Without all of you...I would not be me.

Honestly and Always,

Nancy Hoppes Sellnau

THANK YOU

To my granddaughter,
MacKenzie Rae Sellnau,
for designing my Cover.
My dear friend,
Greg Bordignon,
for transforming the vision of my
'Turtle Self' into such a fine self-portrait.

MOTHER'S TEARS

A mother's tears shall always fall,
*   on a pillow filled with dreams.*
Then flow into the endless sea,
*   of promises it seems.*

A father sheds no tears at all,
*   lest they think him not a man.*
Yet an ocean flows within his heart,
*   to a sea of dreams and plans.*

Together they have shown me love,
*   and given life their best.*
I'll save a tear from each dear heart,
*   and dreams shall do the rest.*

AS I SIT

As I sit alone in silence,
    trying desperately to write.
I dream of you so far away,
    I'm needing you tonight.

So many things I want to say,
    but where am I to start.
The words are from so deep within,
    they're coming from my heart.

CONCEIVED

Conceived in love we gave you life,
    you made our dreams come true.
I felt you grow beneath my heart,
    I loved and cherished you.

Then came the day I gave you birth,
    the pain I bore with joy.
I looked at you through tears of love,
    He'd given me a boy.

In my arms I held you then,
    when life to you was new.
Such a small and helpless bundle,
    my love would shelter you.

As the weeks and months went by,
    I loved to watch you grow.
I nourished you with food and love,
    you captured my heart so.

Then you learned to coo and smile,
    to scoot, to crawl, to walk.
And if I listened hard enough,
    I was sure I heard you talk.

You grew into your little world,
*   the one that's made for boys.*
The one that's filled with rocks and toads,
*   with trees and trucks and noise.*

Then still another world you faced,
*   the day you went to school.*
The world of books and ABC's,
*   of studying and rules.*

As you're growing older now,
*   with ideas of your own.*
It's hard for you to understand,
*   a world you've never known.*

A world that's filled with promises,
*   that sometimes we can't keep.*
A world of joys to make you smile,
*   or sorrows to make you weep.*

Your worlds will keep on changing,
*   as you grow into a man.*
Just remember that I love you,
*   and I'll help you if I can.*

FRIENDSHIP

Please take my hand and be my friend,
  someone on whom I can depend.
Life is too short to be unkind,
  a friend in all I hope I find.
Walk with me along life's road,
  let us share it's heavy load.

Help me up if I fall down,
  never let me wear a frown.
Encourage me to smile today,
  for through your smile I'll find the way.
Judge me not for things I do,
  for judgment not shall I pass on you.

If I should die before the morrow,
  please let your heart be free from sorrow.
For today you came and took my hand,
  you were a friend to me.
You helped and tried to understand,
  good friends we'll always be.

I HAD TO

I had to stop along my way,
and touch your heart with mine today.

So hold me close and squeeze me tight,
and sleep within my life tonight.

PERHAPS IN SILENCE

How can I possibly tell you how very much you mean to me?

How can I tell you about the warmth that surges through me at just the thought of you?

How can I tell you about the way I want to touch you, the way I need you, the way I love you?

How can I tell you about the me you've found sleeping inside and set free?

How can I tell you about how beautiful you make me feel every time you touch me, every time you make love to me?

How can I tell you about my fantasies, about our world so deep within my heart?

How can I tell you that I love you so deeply, so completely, so honestly?

Perhaps in Silence............

THERE YOU ARE

There you are.....my love:

> *Your eyes seeing into the dark corners of my mind,*

> *Your hand touching my heart,*

> *Your arms sheltering me from pain,*

> *Your smile twinkling in my eyes,*

> *Your existence arousing my desires to be me,*

> *Your strength supporting my weaknesses,*

> *Your courage smothering my fears,*

> *Your love sustaining my life.*

INSENSITIVE

Some are so insensitive,
*   to what we feel inside.*
To what we need or what we want,
*   to what it is called "PRIDE".*

Their hearts have grown so cold...so hard,
*   the business world is theirs.*
You try to tell it like it is,
*   they turn and say "WHO CARES".*

They step on you and put you down,
*   they push you to the end.*
Then turn around and smile at you,
*   and say they are your "FRIEND".*

No credit do they give to you,
*   for work that you have done.*
They never take the time to stop,
*   look back and say "WELL DONE".*

Somehow the world will change them,
*   spinning 'round before their eyes.*
One day you'll turn around and see,
*   they're standing on "YOUR SIDE".*

CHRISTMAS LOVE

Christmastime is a time to give,
   a time to love and a time to live.
A time for cheer and a time for smiles,
   a time to share across the miles.

A time to write to those away,
   and bid them have a happy day.
To tell them what you've done all year,
   and wish that they could all be near.

A time to take another's hand,
   and treat him as your fellow man.
Then keep his hand throughout the year,
   and keep his friendship always near.

A time to take the time to care,
   and show the world there's love to spare.
A time to show both young and old,
   the world outside is not so cold.

A time to put your fears aside,
   and share the joys you hold inside.
A time to pray for peace and love,
   and guidance from the Lord above.

Merry Christmas as this comes your way,
   I hope you have a pleasant day.
Happy New Year too as it rounds the bend,
   it's always nice to have a friend.

MY MAN

I have a man that loves me,
    much more than words can say.
And he takes the time to show it,
    no matter what the day.

Each morning as I awaken,
    and turn to kiss his cheek.
Love's sunshine beams within me,
    there's no need for us to speak.

The love we share so honestly,
    has grown throughout the years.
It all has come so naturally,
    through joy...and sometimes tears.

We never hold back what we feel,
*   in good times...or in bad.*
We take each day as given us,
*   and cherish what we've had.*

Today is tomorrow's memory,
*   tomorrow is but a dream.*
Our love is like a fallen leaf,
*   just floating down life's stream.*

It sometimes stops along the way,
*   to lie in the warmth of the sun.*
And then again it rushes on,
*   as though it's just begun.*

LOVE TO ME

Love to me...is you,
the things you say and the things you
do.

The way you are and the way you'll be,
your love is all my eyes can see.

CHRISTMAS GIFT

Your Christmas gift has given me,
*   not a material thing somehow it must be.*

Not something that's seen on a shelf in a store,
*   but love from your heart to me means much*
*   more.*

Loving me...lifting me...showing you care,
*   to this love... objects can't compare.*

Understanding what makes me the way that I am,
*   and loving me anyway from whence we began.*

Accepting whatever my life has to give,
*   and facing the challenge within me to live.*

Not something that's seen on a shelf in a store,
*   but love from your heart to me means much more.*

SILENCE

I lay in silence dreaming,
*   of the times that we have shared.*
The times that we have slipped away,
*   and shown how much we cared.*

I dream of what you mean to me,
*   how real our love has grown.*
So strong and warm and beautiful,
*   so many ways it's shown.*

I dream I see you standing there,
*   so warm, so strong, so tall.*
I come to you with everything,
*   I give to you my all.*

RETIRING

Retiring...giving up those tasks in life,
that are felt to be a chore.
And looking to the pleasant side...
to things you like much more.

No alarm clocks set on Monday,
as the crack of dawn draws near.
Just your morning coffee perking,
such a pleasant sound to hear.

A nice warm morning shower,
Love's warm smile to start your day.
A quiet morning breakfast...
are you ready...you're on your way.

All those things you've set aside,
'til you had "a bit more time".
They're sitting there...just waiting,
getting mellow like fine wine.

Now you'll have the time for them,
at your leisure...one by one.
Even those you've dreaded most,
just might turn out to be fun.

A little rest...a lot of fun,
much love and worlds of pleasure.
New experiences join the old ones,
wrapped in memories you will treasure.

DREAMS

So clearly in my dreams last night,
    I felt you lying there.
Your skin so warm against my breast,
    loves moonlight in your hair.

In silence how I loved you,
    within my world of dreams.
Your love so deep within me,
    how real it always seems.

How sensuous you make me feel,
    such fantasies I spin.
How naturally the mornings dawn,
    will let us love again.

WITHIN

The love we hold within our hearts,
means so much more to me.
Than what I've ever been in life,
or what I'll ever be.

NAKED

You've never seen me naked,
  you can't say that I'm not fat.
You've never seen me naked,
  in nothing but a hat.

I can hide the bumps and bulges,
  with frills and lace and flowers.
I can suck it in and hold it in,
  be miserable for hours!

I'd like to gain some self-control,
  a system must be found.
To stop this endless battle,
  of bulges, bumps and pounds.

Sugar is my enemy,
  it seems to have the power.
To push, to pull and test my will
  every minute, every hour.

I know the answer lies within
  the chambers of my heart.
I deserve to let myself succeed,
  tomorrow is my start.

HOLD A PLACE

Hold a place for me in the quiet corners of your mind.

Whisper to me softly....in silence.

Caress me tenderly....among the crowds.

Think of me....and love me in the midst of a trying day.

DAWN

Wake up now....stop your dreaming,
*   reality waits for you.*
The cycle of life continues on,
*   there's nothing you can do.*

Lamenting will not change things,
*   it's the way life has to be.*
So blink your eyes....stop staring,
*   face the world and you will see.*

Life continues on....without,
*   some of those that you held dear.*
But in your mind are memories,
*   to keep them ever near.*

Don't pull yourself within you,
*   sinking deeper till you're lost.*
It was just another bridge in life,
*   it's best now that it's crossed.*

PUDD'N

My daddy called me Pudd'n...
        he always loved me so.
I was born when he was 28...
        he died when I was 28.
I always called him DADDY...
        I'll always love him so.

GRAMPA

Not old enough are we as yet,
*   to know the ways of life...or death.*
But the love you showed us during our
*   few short years shall sustain us...*
*   and maintain our many happy*
*   memories of you.*

*   Wesley 12*
*   Sharon 11*
*   David   10*
*   Kurt   8*
*   Brian   7 1/2*
*   Jennifer 2 1/2*
and

Brenda 2 1/2 months - Never have my blue
eyes been seen by yours...nor my stubby
little nose, my fat little cheeks, my little
double chin and my tiny mouth. All of
these were gifted to me as mommy
confirmed my conception on the day of
your passing. Her love for you shall forever
embrace my heart.

WIDE AWAKE

Somewhere between wide-awake and dreaming...

I lay and think of how very much you mean to me.

LITTLE SOMETHING

Just a little something,
with a note along today.
To let you know you're thought of,
in a very special way.

AS I

As I cared about you,
I found I cared for you.

As I felt your needs,
I found I needed you.

As I felt your love,
I found I loved you.

TEARS

Tears trickle down the cheeks of Mom,
a sniffle comes from Dad.
They flashback on your years of youth,
such pleasures they have had.

Memories of the very first time,
they held you in their arms.
And how you always made things right,
with that special little boy charm.

So proud are they of how you've grown,
how you've become a man.
The qualities you've shown to all,
reflect their guiding hand.

Now the time has come for you,
to start another life.
Thus friends and family gather round,
as love becomes your wife.

Hand in hand you're standing there,
*   as you pledge your vows of love.*
The star of love shines down on you,
*   with blessings from above.*

As you step down from the altar,
*   hand in hand your hearts are one.*
The isle of life in front of you,
*   your world has just begun.*

Tears trickle down the cheeks of Mom,
*   a sniffle comes from Dad.*
From love they've gained a daughter,
*   many pleasures to be had.*

HOW LONG

I used to lay and wonder,
how long this love would last.
How long before you tired of me,
and put me in your past.

Then you made me realize,
your love for me was real.
A love of warm sweet honesty,
how wonderful it feels.

Now I never worry,
if the end shall ever come.
For I know down deep inside your heart,
you will always love me some.

True love never turns to hate,
passions cool...but never die.
Just let us love from deep within,
and never question why.

JOEL PAUL

Days filled with bright, warm sunshine,
*   a home that's filled with love.*
A family now united,
*   all sheltered from above.*

Love, peace and understanding,
*   good health and new found joy.*
God has shown His light upon you,
*   and blessed you with a boy.*

Joel Paul you now shall christen him,
*   with friends and family near.*
God's love abounds within us,
*   and glistens in a tear.*

I CARE

I care about what you are and what you'll be,
    where you're coming from and where you're
    going.
I care how you feel inside....what you're thinking,
    what you need and what you want.....I love you.

I need you to make me feel warm inside,
    I need to care about you and to love you.
I have a need to be a whole person....
    an individual with ideas and opinions of my own....
    and not be afraid to express them.
I need you to care enough to let me be me...
    to need me, to want me, and to love me..

PATIENCE

God grant me the Patience.....

To let my children	**P**lay
to let them	**A**nger
and to let them	**T**ease
To let my children	**I**ndulge
to let them	**E**ncounter
and to let them	**N**avigate
To let my children	**C**aptivate
to let them	**E**NJOY

And most of all.....to let them be
CHILDREN....
for they shall have time enough to be
*Grown-Up and be **PATIENT**.*

I'm Just A Child

I saw the look in your eyes....
I heard the tone of your voice.
I didn't mean to disappoint you....
I'm just a child.

I know how much you love me....
I know how much you care.
I know I need your guidance....
I'm just a child.

I promise to try harder....
I promise to do better.
But if I sometimes falter,
please remember....
I'm just a child.

PEACEFUL

It's peaceful here among the trees,
as I sit here all alone.
Joined only by a silent breeze,
and memories all my own.

Memories of the love we've shared,
a love that keeps on growing.
Memories of the times we've shared,
and didn't mind it showing.

WRAP YOURSELF

Wrap yourself around me...
and make me warm.

Feel yourself within me...
and give me love.

Caress my heart...
for from it comes my life....
filled with loving you, wanting you,
and needing you.

WHAT IF

What if what I'm running to,
is what I'm running from.

And all that I would leave behind,
is only yet to come.

YOUR EYES

As I looked into your warm brown eyes,
      I saw myself looking back at me.
What was it I expected,
      what did I hope to see?

I saw the love I gave to you,
      explode inside your heart.
Then shower down surrounding me,
      as from the very start.

YOUR LIGHT

The more I try to guide you,
the more you turn away.
It seems the more I think of you,
the less I know to say.

I'm only trying to help you,
and be there as a friend.
Perhaps it's less you need from me,
and more from deep within.

Decisions must be made by you,
I see they can't be mine.
For you're the one to gain or lose,
it's your time now to shine.

Whatever be your path in life,
I'll be right by your side.
Trying not to push or shove,
but sharing in your pride.

TOMORROWS

*May all of your tomorrows blossom into
bright, sunny today's ...*

*then fade into the shadows of beautiful,
peaceful memories.*

MARRIAGE

Always Remember

Only

True Commitment

Wrapped in the arms of

Respect and Trust

Laid down as a foundation

and held in place by

Honesty and Communication

can be crowned as

LOVE

And become a truly

LASTING MARRIAGE

MORE

The more I look at you,
*   the more I see you.*
The more I touch you,
*   the more I feel you.*
The more I have you,
*   the more I want you.*
The more you offer me,
*   the more I want to give you.*
The more you take from me,
*   the more you give of yourself.*

AUTUMN

The leaves of Fall surround me,
reaching deep within my heart.
With colors of the world around,
of which I am a part.

My spirits rise, my soul awakens,
my heart begins to pound,
Thoughts filled with precious memories,
God's blessings all around.

IN SEARCH OF ME

So deep within the heart of me,
*   I find myself still sleeping.*
Then gently stirred by life around,
*   I lay in silence weeping.*
So much more I want from life,
*   than what I've come to be.*
So many things I want to do,
*   so much I want to see.*
So many things I've never tried,
*   I've never had the time.*
But time shall never come to me,
*   unless myself I find.*
My life has never been my own,
*   the blame is all on me.*
I've never been just by myself,
*   to see what I could be.*
I've always been so insecure,
*   afraid to be alone.*
Afraid to face the world myself,
*   and tackle the unknown.*
I've never let my voice be heard,
*   or taken a strong stand.*
For what if someone disagreed,
*   or didn't understand.*
But here I am within myself,
*   a person with a name.*
I have a right to live my life,
*   or not to play the game.*

DESPAIR

I know that you can't comprehend,
can't truly understand.

The depth of darkness and despair,
that sometimes holds my hand.

SPECIAL

It's a very special person,
*   the one that my eyes see.*
The one that tries to understand,
*   and is a friend to me.*

There are times when another's confidence,
*   can help to pull us through.*
This you've given unto me,
*   when friends have seemed so few.*

I've put you in the middle,
*   and it helps to see you there.*
So many never take the time,
*   or seem to really care.*

It's a very special person,
*   the one that my eyes see.*
The one that tries to understand,
*   and is a friend to me.*

SNOWFLAKES

As I stand alone in darkness,
*   snowflakes gently kiss my face.*
The star of love shines down on me,
*   with brilliance and with grace.*

Feel not the cold around you,
*   but the warmth within your heart.*
Alone we stand together,
*   even though we're far apart.*

We stand alone in darkness,
*   snowflakes gently kiss our face.*
The star of love shines down on us,
*   with brilliance and with grace.*

ANNIVERSARY LOVE

Thirty-five years have come and gone
*   since the day you spoke your vows.*
So very much has come to pass,
*   between that day and now.*

You started out with only love,
*   in a time so full of hate.*
You rose together to face each day,
*   of a life just hinged on fate.*

You've worked together side by side,
*   in good times and in bad.*
You take life as it's given you,
*   and cherish what you've had.*

Your children, as you look at them,
*   look back through eyes of love.*
For the love and warmth you've given them,
*   was sheltered from above.*

Gradually they've grown and gone,
*   to be out on their own.*
Then taken each a mate to love,
*   and start another home.*

So thus by four your family grew,
  and then by four plus two.
Now all the love that fills their hearts,
  reflects itself on you.

Just sit back now and rest a while,
  from all that you've been through.
And let this be a special time,
  for just the two of you.

Let the star of love shine down,
  to brighten each new day.
And let you know we love you both,
  much more than words can say.

SOMEDAY

Someday I will be...
         better than...
         brighter than...
         prettier than...
         thinner than...
         taller than...
         happier than...
         smarter than...
But for today...I will be me!

FREE TIME 1978

My job takes the freshest part of my day and I take pride in giving 100% plus to do my job well. My efforts are appreciated and I feel that I am paid justly.

In commuting from rural Martelle, IA to Cedar Rapids, IA, I am away from home 10 ½ to 11 hours a day. My family only gets 4 ½ to 5 hours of my time, and that 4 ½ to 5 hours is after a busy day at work. Naturally, I feel they are somewhat cheated. However, the children grow and never complain. My husband has a tired, frazzled wife – so isn't he a little cheated too? But would I be any less tired after a busy day at home? I don't know. What about me – am I cheated? I've missed so many of those precious moments that can never be recaptured – the ones the babysitter tells you about when you get home – the ones the paycheck just doesn't seem to make up for. I missed the Halloween party and the Christmas program. The boys said they understood. They say, "I know you can't come, but there's a music program on Wednesday." Aren't they being cheated?

My husband works too, isn't he missing the same things that I am? We farm 80 acres, but 80 acres cannot pay for itself and support a family too, so my husband and I both work outside the home – is it worth it? Progress – are we progressing or falling behind?

I always question the term "FREE TIME". I always just need "MORE TIME". If I had time enough to keep my house as neat and clean as I'd like to, my mending done and my family happy, then any time left over perhaps would be "FREE TIME". The time I use to write poetry, read, sew, or go shopping always seems like "BORROWED TIME". It's time I feel should be spent mending jeans, cleaning cupboards, straightening drawers, or weeding the garden. I usually end up making myself feel guilty about the time I'm taking, "just for me". All time has a value, I feel selfish if I misuse it. Does life really offer "FREE TIME"?

THOUGHTS and REFLECTIONS
OF THE HEART

Only the light from within can truly brighten your day...Let it Shine!

You call me a Little Girl...
treat me like a Lady...
and make me feel like a Woman!

How warm and tender our love has grown...
no greater love than one that's shown.

Whisper softly that you love me...
hear the echo in my heart.

So many beautiful things can never be said...just felt...in moments of tender, sweet silence.

As you gaze into the flickering embers...
I shall come to you...and love you.

---

*Time is for caring about those around
you....smile and take the time.*

*Like rays of sunshine bursting through the
morning's dawn... let me brighten your day
and fade into your night...into your dreams.*

*Sometimes we feel so deeply that there are
no words to convey how we feel...out of the
depths of silence shall flow the strongest
feelings of love.*

*There is nowhere you can run to that is as
important as where you are.*

*As I lay dreaming...listening to the chilling
winter rain.
I feel your presence surrounding
me...warming me...loving me.*

*Gifts to show how much we care,
          can't be found in any store.
Just giving love and sharing love,
          somehow means so much more.*

Touch me...Hold me...Love me...
make the rest of the world go away,
if only for a little while.

Let me love you in my dreams tonight,
*   let me hold you in my heart.*
Let our love bring us together,
*   even though we're far apart.*

When the world around me gets me down,
*   life seems too much to bear.*
I close my eyes and see your face,
*   your love is always there.*

As I love you....I see love,
As I touch you....I feel you
As I think of you....your love surrounds me,
As I dream of you....your love fulfills me.

Each moment of your life you face a new
situation.
Each new situation offers you an
opportunity.
An opportunity to pass Judgment...
or to exercise your ability to be
Compassionate.

GOD wrapped HIS arm around my shoulder
and whispered....
WE can do this....Not I can do this....Not You
can do this...
but WE can do this.

I'm not asking GOD to take care of me,
I pray that HE will show me how to take
care of myself.

Sometimes the words between the lines are
the ones that speak to me.

In true friendship it matters not whether or
not I need your advice...
only that you care enough to offer it
without judgment.

The total fulfillment of a dream brings an
end to the
excitement of having the dream to reach
for.

Absence is to love like wind is to fire.

Nothing you will do can make me love you more...
Nothing you have done can make me love you less.

There sits gramma in her rocker,
as she sips her cup of tea.
Crocheting one more doily,
making memories for me.

Somewhere between wide-awake and dreaming....
I lay and think of how very much you mean to me.

Bad Day? Hug it off!

LOVE IS...The ability and willingness to
allow those that you
care for to be what they choose for
themselves...without
any insistence that they satisfy you.

Humanitarian Power - The Power of US

57

It's not about Me...It's not about You...It's about US.

It is what it is.....NO.....It is what we make it!

Don't let your past spoil your "here and now" or rob you of your future. Forgive what needs to be forgiven - let go of the pain and grab your happiness before it is too late. Tomorrow is not promised - savor the moment with a Happy Heart. Choose JOY.

THE LITTLE GIRL

The little girl inside of me

has been watching all these years.

Recalling all the memories....

wiping all the tears.

Waiting for those painful thoughts

that haunted me for years.

To be blinded by forgiveness....

quelling all my fears.

Forgiveness came...

my soul awakens...

my heart still beats.

I am free...I choose JOY

MY HEART STILL BEATS

My Soul awakens....

My Heart still beats....

Anyway.

Nancy Hoppes Sellnau